I0755011

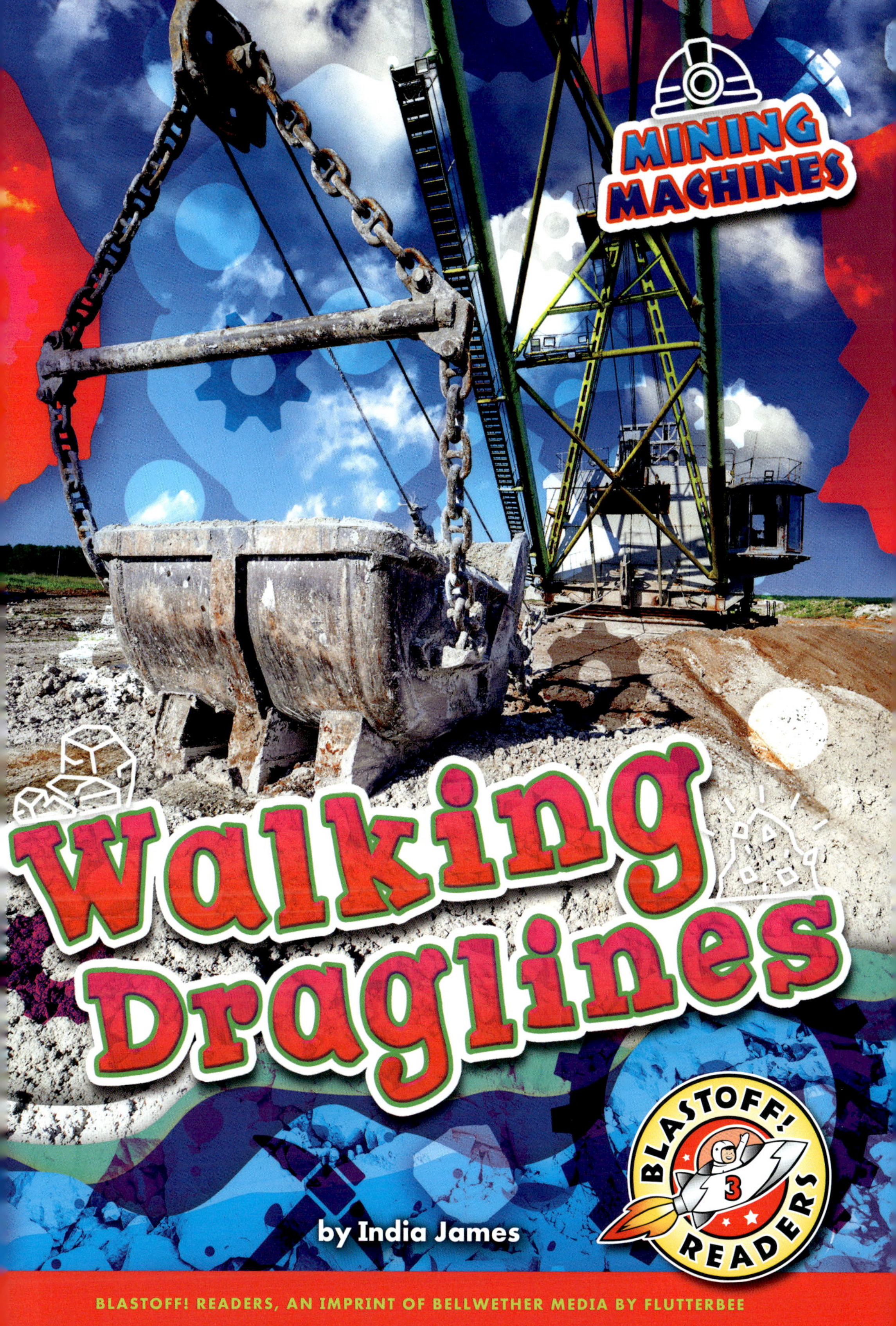
MINING MACHINES
Walking Draglines
by India James
BLASTOFF! READERS 3
BLASTOFF! READERS, AN IMPRINT OF BELLWETHER MEDIA BY FLUTTERBEE

Blastoff! Readers are carefully developed by literacy experts to build reading stamina and move students toward fluency by combining standards-based content with developmentally appropriate text.

LEVELS

Level 1 provides the most support through repetition of high-frequency words, light text, predictable sentence patterns, and strong visual support.

Level 2 offers early readers a bit more challenge through varied sentences, increased text load, and text-supportive special features.

Level 3 advances early-fluent readers toward fluency through increased text load, less reliance on photos, advancing concepts, longer sentences, and more complex special features.

★ **Blastoff! Universe**

Reading Level

Grade K

Grades 1–3

Grade 4

This edition first published in 2027 by Bellwether Media, Inc.

For information regarding permission, write to Bellwether Media, Inc., Attention: Permissions Department, 3500 American Blvd W, Suite 150, Bloomington, MN 55431.

Library of Congress Cataloging-in-Publication Data is available at www.loc.gov or upon request from the publisher.

ISBN: 9798898800734 (hardcover)
ISBN: 9798898801977 (ebook)

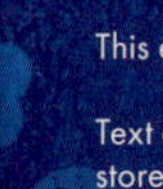

Editor: Kieran Downs   Designer: Jeffrey Kollock

Printed in the United States of America, North Mankato, MN.

Table of Contents

What Are Walking Draglines?

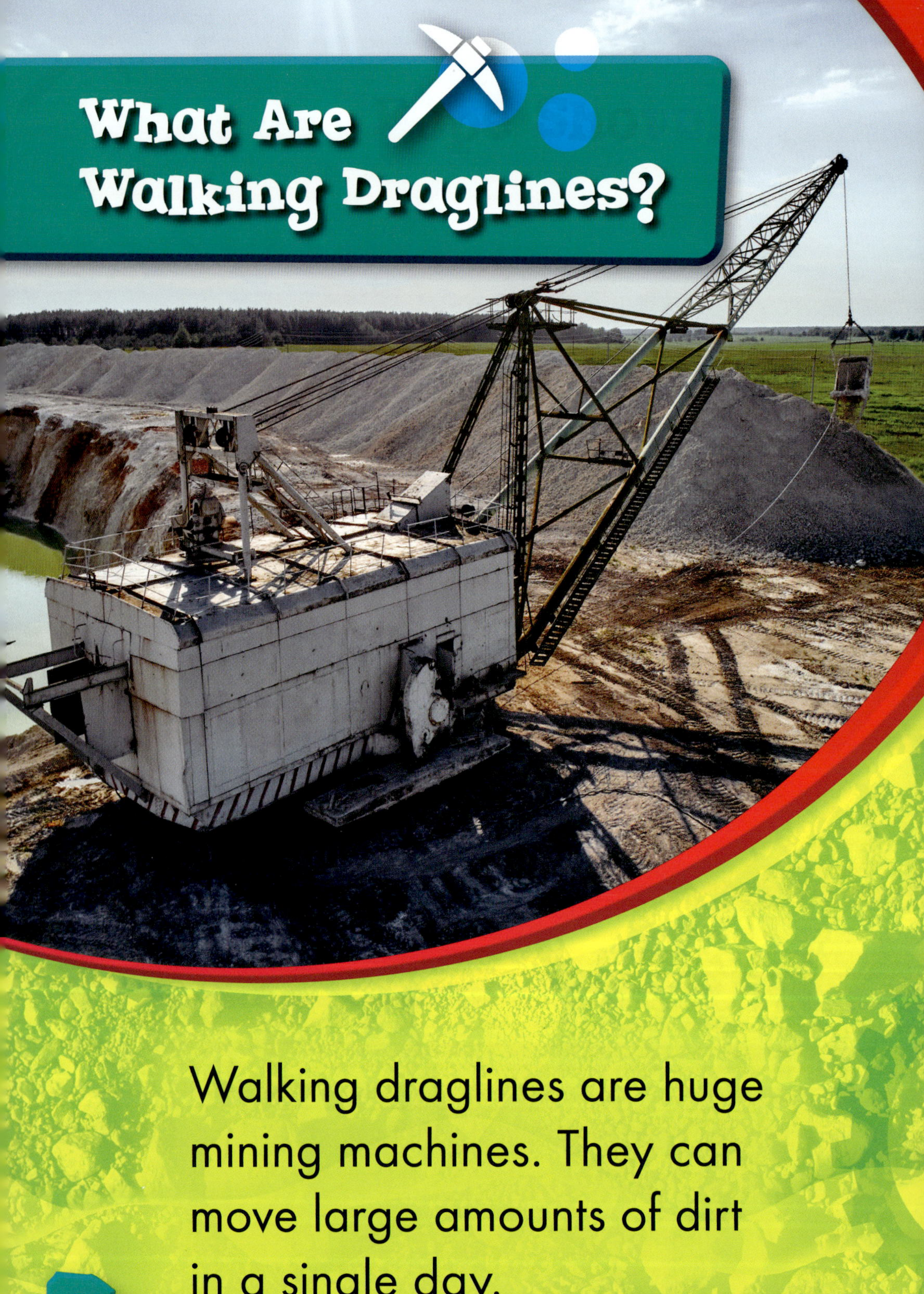

Walking draglines are huge mining machines. They can move large amounts of dirt in a single day.

These machines use cables to pull a bucket. The bucket on the walking dragline scoops up dirt and **ore**.

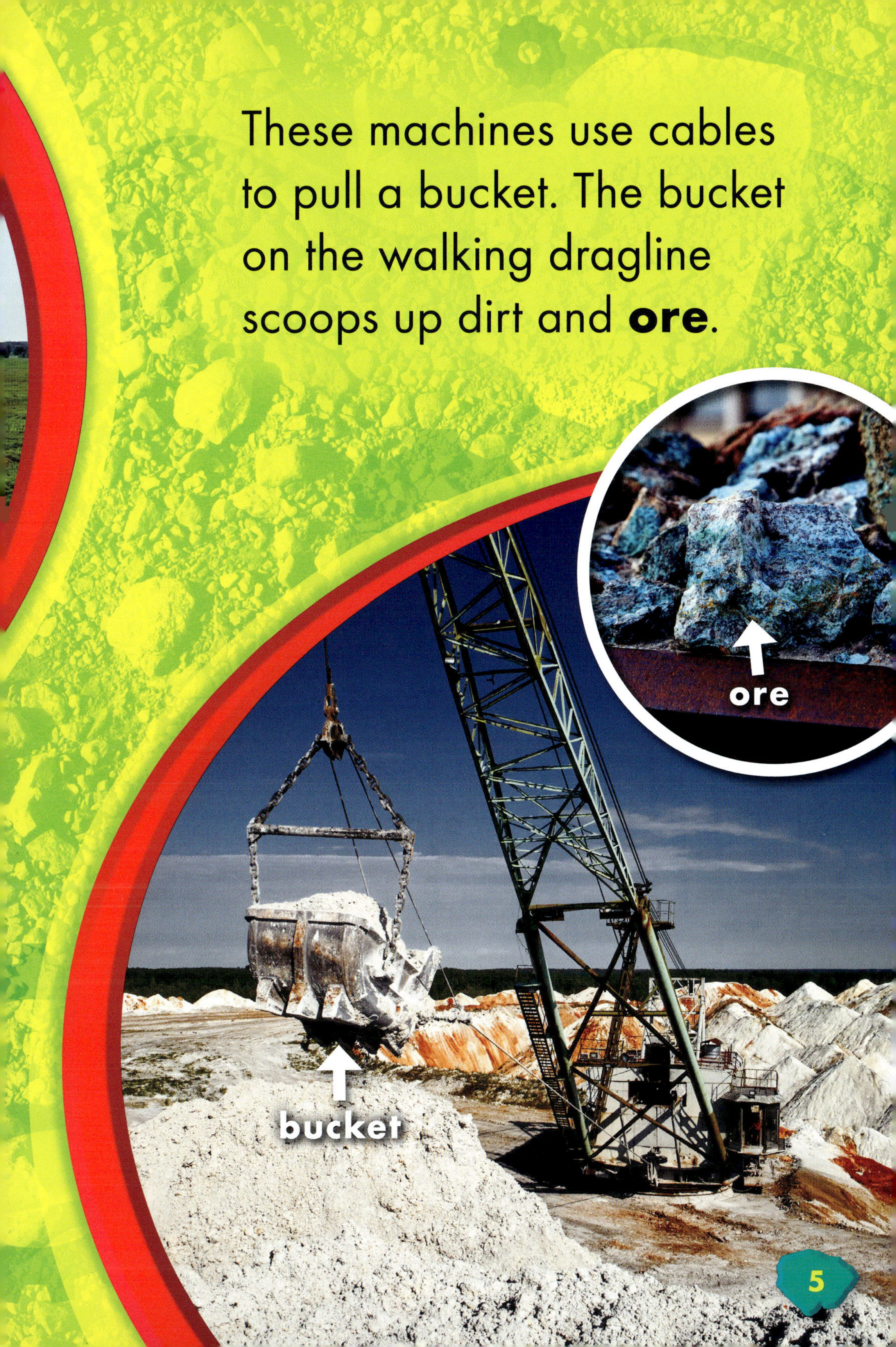

Walking draglines are used in **surface mines**. They are also used in **pit mines**. They are often used to clear **overburden**.

Walking draglines can also be used to dig underwater.

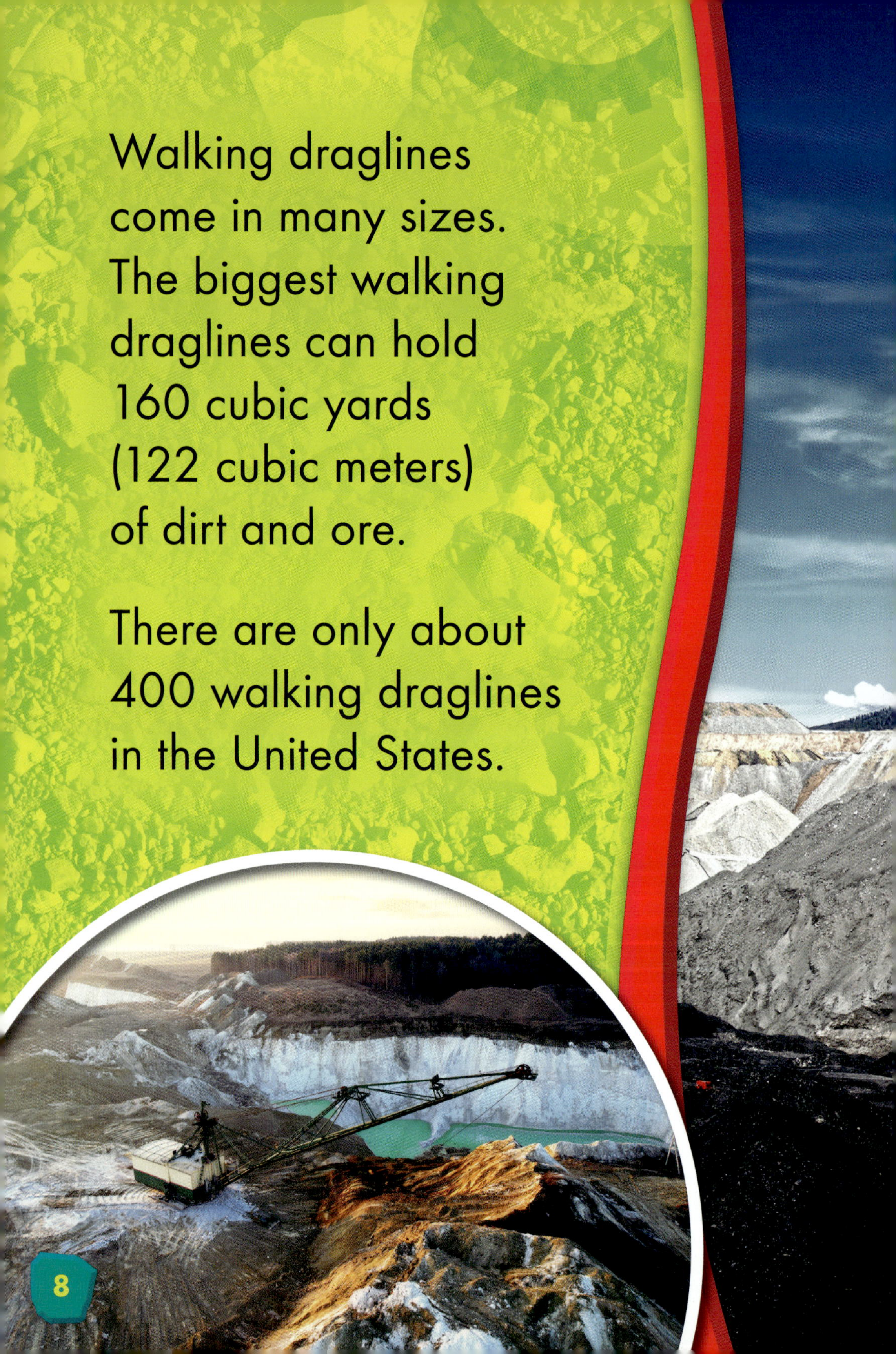

Walking draglines come in many sizes. The biggest walking draglines can hold 160 cubic yards (122 cubic meters) of dirt and ore.

There are only about 400 walking draglines in the United States.

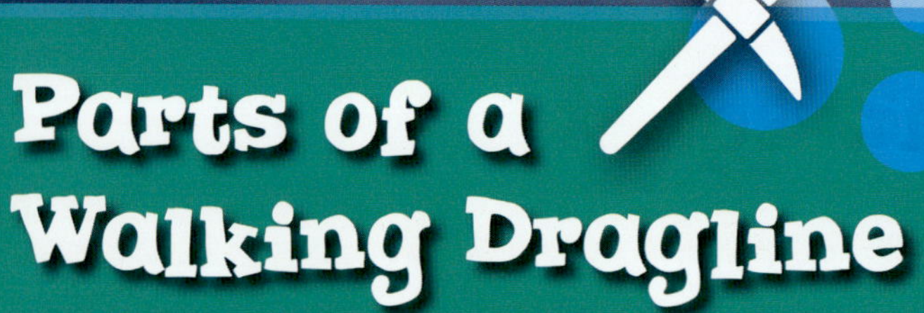

Parts of a Walking Dragline

Walking draglines lift and pull buckets with cables. These help the buckets scoop up dirt.

Drag cables move the buckets forward and backward. **Hoist cables** make the buckets go up and down.

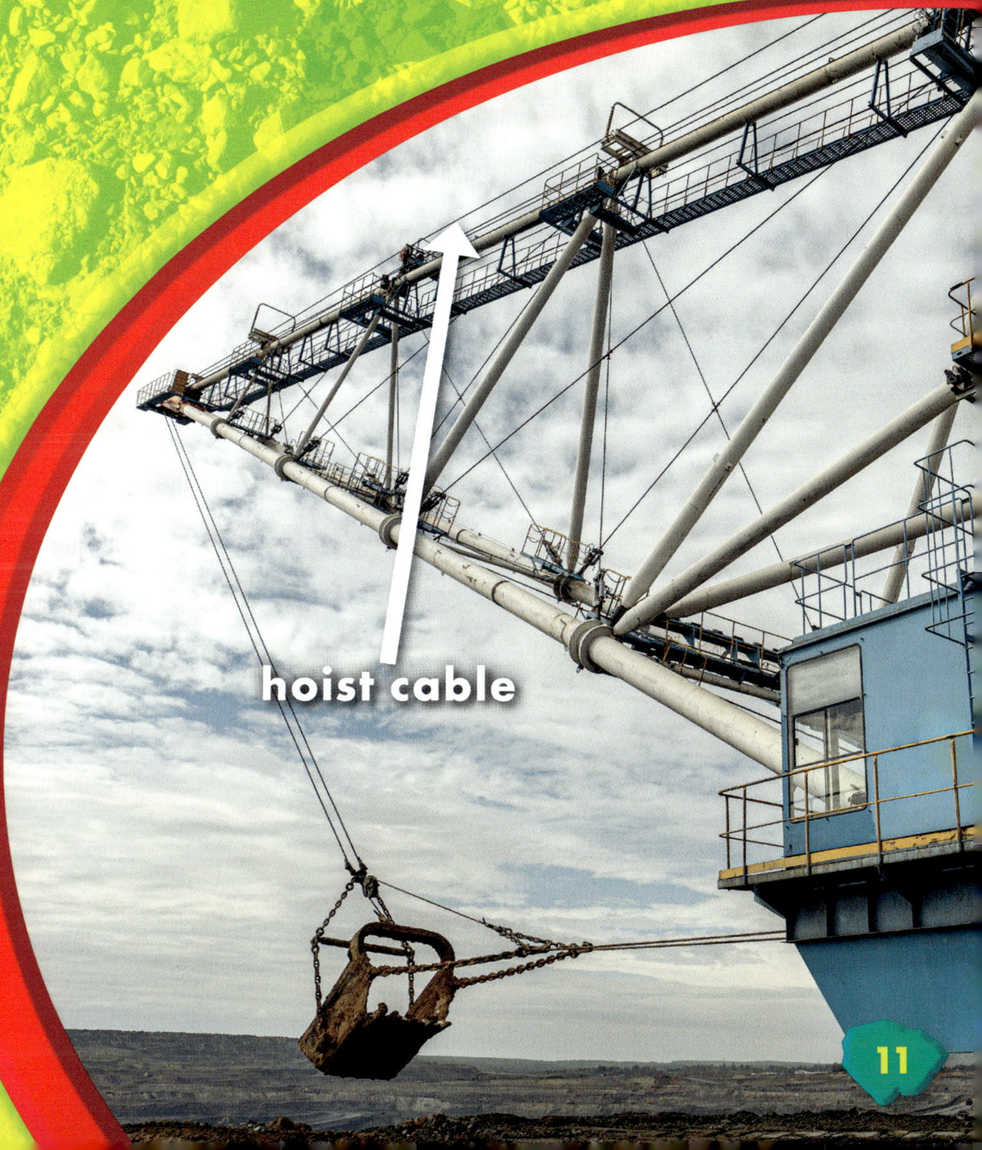

hoist cable

Some walking draglines have two **cabs**. One cab is on the right. The other is on the left.

The driver uses one cab at a time. The driver changes cabs depending on where they are digging.

Walking draglines use feet to move. The feet move up and down.

They move to different parts of the mine. They can move many miles between the places they need to be.

Walking Draglines at Work

Walking draglines take three people to run. One person watches to keep cables away from **obstacles**.

The **oiler** keeps the moving parts working. The driver moves the bucket from inside the cab.

obstacles

Walking draglines move overburden into piles. Dump trucks move the overburden away from the dig site.

Excavators work with walking draglines. They dig where walking draglines cannot reach.

Walking draglines are huge machines. They help keep mines up and running. They help us get ore that we need.

Walking Dragline Profile

Big Muskie

weighed 29.1 million pounds (13.2 million kilograms)

could move 716,500 pounds (325,000 kilograms)

bucket size was 220 cubic yards (168 cubic meters)

Walking draglines are important mining machines!

Glossary

cabs—the parts of a walking dragline where the driver sits

drag cables—cables on a walking dragline that move the bucket forward and backward

hoist cables—cables on a walking dragline that lift the bucket up and down

obstacles—objects that stand in the way

oiler—a worker that keeps the moving parts of a walking dragline working

ore—a valuable material that occurs naturally in the earth

overburden—materials that cover valuable ore

pit mines—mines that get materials from deep, open holes

surface mines—mines that get materials from dirt near Earth's surface

To Learn More

AT THE LIBRARY

James, India. *Mining Shovels.* Minneapolis, Minn.: Bellwether Media, 2027.

James, Ryan. *Excavators.* New York, N.Y.: Crabtree Publishing, 2025.

Rogers, Marie. *Huge Earthmovers.* New York, N.Y.: PowerKids Press, 2022.

ON THE WEB

FACTSURFER

Factsurfer.com gives you a safe, fun way to find more information.

1. Go to www.factsurfer.com.
2. Enter "walking draglines" into the search box and click 🔍.
3. Select your book cover to see a list of related content.

Index

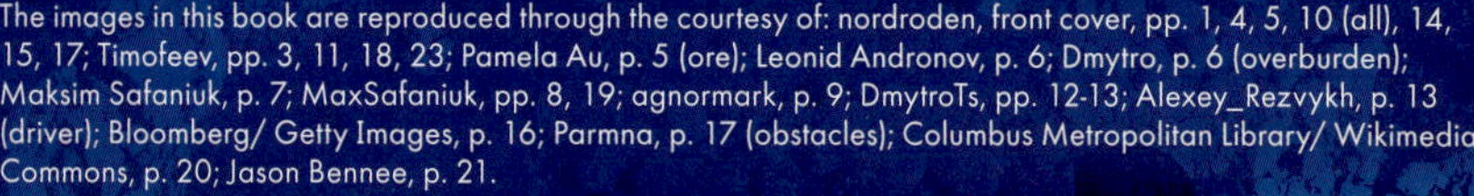
The images in this book are reproduced through the courtesy of: nordroden, front cover, pp. 1, 4, 5, 10 (all), 14, 15, 17; Timofeev, pp. 3, 11, 18, 23; Pamela Au, p. 5 (ore); Leonid Andronov, p. 6; Dmytro, p. 6 (overburden); Maksim Safaniuk, p. 7; MaxSafaniuk, pp. 8, 19; agnormark, p. 9; DmytroTs, pp. 12-13; Alexey_Rezvykh, p. 13 (driver); Bloomberg/ Getty Images, p. 16; Parmna, p. 17 (obstacles); Columbus Metropolitan Library/ Wikimedia Commons, p. 20; Jason Bennee, p. 21.